POPLAR LEAVES
AND SEAWEED

BY

C. C. MARTINDALE, S.J.

LONDON

SHEED & WARD

1940

MADE IN GREAT BRITAIN
BY PURNELL AND SONS, LTD.
PAULTON (SOMERSET) AND LONDON
FIRST PUBLISHED SEPTEMBER 1940
BY SHEED AND WARD, LTD.
FROM 31 PATERNOSTER ROW
LONDON, E.C.4

To

VERONICA SPENCER-BULL

and her Associates

Who so long and gallantly
have worked in Poplar:
If the work was in part a Cross,
a Cross too was its Crown,
" Pro Ecclesia et Pontifice ",
and was well-earned.

APOLOGIA

Some apologia for the following pages may be permitted, lest they seem too much of a doggerel hotch-potch.

For well over ten years we have admired and loved the Settlement of the Holy Child in Poplar, and we thought there was no harm in congratulating it also in childish ways—after all, it *is* the Schools of the Congregation of the Holy Child which are responsible for it—nor did we hesitate to ask leave from Messrs. Sheed and Ward to include here a few verses from " Gospel Rhymes " which, though they have nothing directly to do with Poplar, were certainly meant for children. But the Congregation of the Holy Child Jesus has also its own African Mission, in Calabar. This explains allusions to that part of the Black World in some of the songs.

Now the Missionary Sisters could not so much as reach their destination without the help of Seamen; so, since we are independently devoted to the Apostleship of the Sea, we determined to add some " Seaweed " to the Poplar Leaves, and anyhow they reminded us of pleasant days, and of better still than that. In fact, we could not keep ourselves from including some pages reprinted from *The Month* (Oct., 1931) with its Editor's kind permission. Despite their possible eccentricity,

they are a transcript of experience, and if the in-
genious reader cares to take some trouble, he can
trace in them a good many guiding *motifs*, so to
say—oh well, for example the Sea-bird, the Stokers'
cages, and the Dove. Anyhow, our word must be
taken that it does mean something.

But further, Poplar is a river-side district and
sends a good many boys and men to sea; and from
the Settlement windows and its club-roof you look
across " Cut-Throat Lane ", coal-dumps and a
railway to warehouses between which you see the
funnels and the derricks of West India Docks,
while just beyond the Settlement you come to
Blackwall Tunnel and the East India Docks. This
encouraged us to add also some verses upon the
Limehouse church which overlooks the Thames;
and this in its turn drew after it one or two more
songs about London churches of which overseas
visitors, like ourselves, are fond—songs that we
wrote in hours of sickness for the *Catholic Herald*,
which, like *The Pylon*, we thank for permission to
re-print.

We say " songs ", because much of what follows
has been put to music by Mr. Bernard Merefield,
music which would have been too expensive to
print, especially since at our obstinate request he
inserted some rather startling harmonies—or dis-
sonances—which seemed to us suitable not least
for " What's o'clock in Poplar? " But his music

is always robust and joyous and we hope that it may again be sung inside or out of the Holy Child schools.

Four songs were admittedly cribbed from the Harrow Song-book—" St. George ", " The Cardinal is Coming ", " Here, Sir ", and " Queen Elizabeth ". But they were wholly re-written— the last two for a number of boys emigrating to Flock House in New Zealand, an admirable institution founded for the agricultural and farm training of sons of seamen killed or gravely injured in the War. We like to register our gratitude for so many loyal and affectionate friendships. The first and last sets of verses are meant as it were to enclose the others in a Eucharistic framework; and we hope that many readers will remember Poplar, Calabar, and the Apostleship of the Sea at the Holy Sacrifice and in their Communions. So this poor little collection has its serious background.

CONTENTS

xi

POPLAR LEAVES AND SEAWEED

THREE MASSES

The School Chapel

"HOLY ! Holy ! Holy ! " Chime it not so
  slowly !
  Hasten, Lord, the splendid hour when Thou dost
    mount Thy throne !
Lord, for Thee the roses breathe their heart out
    wholly:
  Lord, the candles burn away their lives for Thee
    alone.
" Holy, Holy, Holy ! " Incense rising slowly;
  Purest linen, purest pearl adorn Thine altar-
    throne:
All our best to Thee, Lord, consecrated solely;
  All the loveliest gifts of life we will to be Thine
    own.

Poplar

" Kyrie, eleison ! " Broken, bruised and lonely,
  Tired before the day can dawn, O Christ, we
    creep to Thee.
Where shall we find mercy, save in Jesus only ?
  Where, a Heart to understand the hearts of such
    as we ?
Bread of Life—bewildered whence to find our
    living—

Crimson Vine—we stumble, faint and drained of
half our blood.
Water, cool and cleansing—Fount of free for-
giving—
Life of our exhausted life, 'tis *Thou* hast understood.

Calabar

" Blessed! Benedictus! " Thou from heavenly glory
All the way to Calabar hast not disdained to
come!
All the jungle-voices join to sing the story;
Once again the palms are strewn to give Thee
welcome home.
Thou from fields of deathless flowers hast come—
so lowly—
Little snow-white Lamb of God, to shepherd
even me.
Skies and rains and rivers chant Thy" Holy, Holy!"
See! We lift in Calabar our Eucharist to Thee!

All the World

" Missa est." 'Tis ended. Heaven with earth is
blended;
All the lands of all the earth become Thine altar-
stone.
Yet the song of Sanctus rises up unended;
Yet the Vine of Life is rich with clusters still
ungrown.

4

Word of God, be spoken! Bread from Heaven, be
broken!
Dove divine, Thy pinions spread beyond the
farthest sea!
Dawn of Truth, enlighten worlds yet unawoken!
Praise to Father! praise to Son! Blest Spirit
praise to Thee!

II

WELCOME-SONG[1]

GOOD folk, forsake your houses,
And flock to Poplar Hall—
A joyous message rouses
The hearts of one and all.
O raindrops, cease your strumming!
O skies, be bright and gay—
    The Cardinal is coming
    To visit us to-day! (*repeat.*)

The afternoon is over—
The time for toil is done.
From Inverness to Dover,
Good people, take your fun.
But *we*, still lighter-hearted,
Must gather round to-day—
    The Cardinal has started—
    Has started on his way! (*repeat as always.*)

Westminster lies behind him;
Trafalgar Square is passed:
Beyond the Bank you'll find him,
And Aldgate's here at last.

[1] Originally addressed to H. E. Cardinal Bourne. We thought, at the time, that the smile with which he—ultimately—listened to it was somewhat wan. But now, years afterwards, we hear that he was very pleased with it. Anyway, the tune was first-rate, being ' lifted, from' the *Harrow Song Book.*

6

Commercial Road is cheering,
As loud as voices may—
    The Cardinal is nearing,
    And who would stop away?

Now round the corner swinging
Behold the motor-car—
Your voices skyward flinging
Salute him, Hip-Hurrah!
The motor-car is driving
With due discretion—SAY!
    The Cardinal's arriving!
    Salute him, Hip-Hurray!

Your Eminence, we've heard of
How much you've got to do.
We couldn't do a third of
The work they pile on you!
So all the more we thank you
For putting off your rest,
    And bidding Poplar rank you
    Not only friend but guest.

We know that you remember
Our life's not always gay:
From June to grim December
You think of us each day.
And that is why so loudly
Our welcome here we sing;
    And humbly and yet proudly
    Kneel down to kiss your Ring.

Well, now the song is finished;
And when we say Goodnight,
Affection undiminished
Shall speed you from our sight.
And, wide-awake or dreaming,
You'll find us loyal still;
Your scarlet mantle gleaming
Shall shield our thoughts from ill.

III

ST. GEORGE OF POPLAR[1]

WHEN time was young and the world was
new,[2]
And the fields were green and the skies were blue,
Saint George came galloping up from the sea,
And he stopped at the foot of a Poplar-tree.
    The road was rough and the road was long;
    The Poplar-tree stood straight and strong;
    St. George cried out: " This'll do for me!
    I'll sit for a bit by the Poplar-tree! "

Chorus : St. George, hooray! St. George, hooroo!
           Mark my words if it don't come true!
           In fight or victory, griefs or joys,
           St. George is the friend of the Poplar boys.

And first did he groom his sturdy steed,
And brought him some water and gave him a feed;
When that was finished, the Saint confessed
That he certainly needed a bit of a rest:
    He unbuckled his belt and his corslet too;
    He stretched his arms; deep breaths he drew.

---

[1] It is only fair to say that this song was sung with immense gusto, because of its admirable tune (*Harrow Song Book*) : it was indeed so constantly and piercingly whistled in streets and workshops that pugilistic encounters were to be feared. Its sentiments, however, were treated with a certain bitter scepticism, because : " There wasn't really dragons in the Thames, Miss, was there ? "

[2] And if you say that *new* doesn't rhyme with *blue*, nor *horse* with *cross*, and so on, well, in Poplar they *do*.

He flung himself down on the starry stems—
When a horrible dragon crawled out of the
Thames!
    Chorus :

St. George sprang up from the grass so green,
For so dreadful a dragon he never had seen.
He patted the neck of the big white horse,
And snatched up his shield with the crimson Cross:
    The Dragon he saw him, and loudly he roared;
    But George gripped tight on his terrible sword.
    And " *Come* on, you Dragon! come *on!* " cried he;
    And he stood with his back to the Poplar-tree.
    Chorus :

The Dragon made at him with claws and with tail;
But the Crimson-Cross Saint wasn't one to turn
pale.
The Dragon came at him with fire and with flame;
But St. George cried loud on the Saving Name.
    The Dragon went panting and peering and
    prowling:
    The Dragon came scowling and growling and
    howling:
    But high St. George his sword heaved he,
    And smote him dead by the Poplar-tree.
    Chorus :

Our fields are hardly so green to-day,
And the smoke has blotted the blue away.

And there isn't much left of the Poplar-tree,
But St. George is here—and so are we.
   And Dragons in plenty sneak out of the mud,
   With poisonous claws and they want our blood.
   But a Poplar lad'll be glad to forge
   A sword that is worthy of great St. George.

Last Chorus :

      St. George, hooray! St. George, hooroo!
      Keen and loyal and clean and true—
      In fights or victories, griefs or joys,
      St. George, be proud of your Poplar boys.

IV

WHAT'S O'CLOCK IN POPLAR?

The Settlement boys'-club shuts at 10 *p.m.*

TEN o'clock!
　　Prayers; and then the last Goodnight.
Out to Cut-Throat Lane, and climb
Up to High Street out of sight.
Footsteps fainter in the slime:
Skinny shoulder; panting lung;
Aching back—and yet, you're young . . .
　　　　Sleep, son, sleep.
　　　　Ten o'clock.

　　　　Twelve o'clock!
Through the twisted twigs a breeze
Whispers restlessly—" Oh yes!
Even in Poplar we have trees—
Vine and fig-tree, Miss, no less!
Not that they bear any fruit—
Couldn't, with *that* earth at root! "
　　　　Try to sleep, Worker!
　　　　Twelve o'clock.

　　　　Two o'clock.
Shunting, clashing, clanking train—
Hot behind the heaps of coal.
River, hissing under rain . . .
" River—in the stoker's hole

Have you *anything* for me—
Going desperate out to sea? "
       Sleep, breaking heart!
       Two o'clock.

       Four o'clock.
On the pavement, to and fro,
Heavy boots. Night's work is done!
Bed for *me* . . . But heavier go
Men with days too swift begun,
Could I—'mid your nursery-toys—
Wake you—" Listen to that noise? "
       Sleep, childhood's heart!
       Four o'clock!

       Six o'clock.
I reluctant in my bed
Turn—" It isn't time for Mass? "
Downy pillow—sleepy head—
Hark! the footsteps pass and pass!
Little Server—candles lit . . .
CHRIST, to Thee I offer it!
       HOLD HIGH YOUR HEARTS !
       Six o'clock.

V

THE YEAST

The Kingdom of Heaven is like to leaven, which a woman took and hid in three measures of meal, until the whole was leavened. Matt. xiii. 33.

REBECCA said to Rachel: " We must hurry up and bake,
For there isn't any bread at all, and hardly any cake!
The men'll want their supper before they go to bed;
And they certainly won't like it if there isn't any bread.

"So take some flour and water, dear, and make a lump of dough,
And put it in the oven, dear, and light the fire below.
I fancy we can make them quite a pleasant little feast—
But oh! whatever else you do, do *not* forget the yeast! "

So little Rachel took the flour, and water too she took,
And made a terrible lot of dough and put it in to cook.
But when she looked to see, it hadn't risen in the least—
For O whatever *do* you think? she *had* forgot the yeast!

Yeast! Yeast! Look—look! See the bubbles
rise!
Yeast! I—sim-ply can't believe my eyes!
Rachel ran and put some yeast in dough that
wasn't bread,
And now she finds the oven's got a lovely loaf
instead!

Lord, I can't do very much, because I am so small;
Still, I *can* do *some*thing, Lord, to help You after
all!
My little pinch of leaven, Lord, my tiny prayer
to You
Can sweeten hearts that love You not and change
them through and through.

VI

NOWHERE TO LAY HIS HEAD

*The foxes have holes, and the birds of the air their nests ;
but the Son of Man hath not where to lay His head. Matt.
viii. 20.*

UP the mountain, on the rocks
    Jesus lays Himself to sleep;
Out the little furry fox,
    Out the nestlings come to peep!

Peeping, creeping, close beside—
    " Look where Jesus goes to rest!
Snuggled in my hole I hide—
    Hasn't Jesus got a nest? "

Lord, the pointed rocks for Thee—
    Lord, for me my cosy bed:
Eiderdown, perhaps, for me—
    Not one pillow for *Thy* head!

Still, I whisper, " Lord, Goodnight!
    Bless the lonely, cold and sad!
Keep them in Thy watchful sight;
    Let me help Thee make them glad! "

VII

NOT ONE GRAIN WAS LOST

Of herself, the Earth bears fruit. Mark iv. 28.

I TOOK my sack of seed;
  I sowed it in my field;
And home I went to reckon up
The harvest it would yield.

When out I went next day
The seed had vanished quite.
Inside the red and crumbly earth
It tucked itself from sight.

Then shone the golden sun,
And lightly fell the rain—
The months went by, I half forgot
How I had thrown the grain.

But one day, forth I fared—
Oh look! where once there'd been
Nothing but dusty lumpy earth,
A shimmering silken green!

Dear Lord, my tiny prayers
I offer You for all
Who need them. It's enough to know
You always hear my call.

17

Whether I pray for Chinamen
Or sailors on the sea,
Or just for poor unhappy folks
Who'll never know it's me—

It doesn't matter, because You
Take care about the grain
I've tried to scatter through the world
For harvest once again.

VIII

THE LILIES OF THE FIELD

Look at the lilies of the field! They toil not, neither do they spin. Yet not Solomon in all his glory was arrayed like one of these! Matt. vi. 28, 29.

WHEN I am living in London Town,
    Mother says: " Darling, it's time for your
    walk! "
People go up, and the people go down—
    Really you *hardly* can hear yourself talk!
Where is the King in his golden crown?
    Couldn't I, *couldn't* I see him?—but OH!
    Look at the hyacinths all in a row!

Home in the country I go for my run
    Over the meadows where daffodils toss
Golden-heads ever so gay in the sun—
    Watch me find violets, shy in the moss!
Mother, don't call me! I haven't quite done
    Making a necklace all rosy and green—
    Rubies and emeralds, fit for the Queen!

Yet none was so royal, dear Jesus, as Thou;
    None was so great or so mighty a King:

But never a glory of gold for Thy brow—
　　Nor for Thy Mother a diamond ring—
Look at the flowers I am bringing Thee now—
　　Bunches of cowslips for Mary to wear—
　　Buttercup coronets bright for her hair!

IX

BABY WHITE-THOUGHTS

O MUMMY darling, pick me up and put me
    on your knee!
I want to tell you something—Yes! I'm going out
    to sea!
So may I have a penny, all the way to Calabar?
I want to see the country where the Other Babies
    are.

  O set your sail and trim your sail, and come to
      Calabar;
  For never rail will get you there, and never
      motor-car!
  The porpoises are tumbling, and the fishes flash
      and fly;
  The very waves are singing because you'll be
      coming by!

My darling little White-Thoughts, aren't you really
    rather wee
To go travelling a-lonely all the way across the sea?
And supposing I came with you, does my tiny baby
    think
I could ever bear to watch her turning black instead
    of pink?

  Unfurl your sail and spread your sail—Nigeria
      isn't far;

And choose your day, a golden day, and come to
Calabar!
The jolly whale is spouting at the thought of you
with glee;
The bright blue skies are bluer 'cause you're
coming out to me!

But, Mummy, I was thinking that you'd come and
help me pack;
And it really wouldn't matter if I *did* get rather
black!
The crocodiles won't eat me if I bring them out
some cake—
But, OH, whatever should I do suppose I met a
snake?

Dear heart, be brave, and breast the wave, though
sinks the Northern Star;
And it isn't always sunshine even here in Calabar.
You'd hardly guess the loneliness, at times,
beneath the trees—
Yes, even when black babies come and perch
upon your knees!

O Baby, Baby White-Thoughts, you must wait a
little while.
But you've made Our Lord so happy, and you've
made His Mother smile.
So put your hands together, and we'll say a Goodnight prayer,

And tell Jesus how you're thinking of the children
    Over There.

    O tiny prayer, on wings of air you've come to
      Calabar!
    O folded fingers, working now where other babies
      are!
    Not far from them lies Bethlehem, nor dimly
      shines its Star—
    The Holy Child is born again out here in
      Calabar.

X

DISTRACTIONS

The Nun :

    Sitting alone in your place by the column—
    Why are you looking so puzzled and solemn?
    Only the red little lamps are a-gleam—
    Where have you gone to? What is your dream?

Pteronoë :

    Oh, I was wondering how I could follow—
    Follow my dear little brown little Swallow;
    Out of the mist and the grey and the cold—
    Out to the blue world—out to the gold!

    Brown little Swallow, O where are you resting?
    " Snug in the chink of a Pyramid nesting!
    Ages ago, did they build it to be
    Home for a little bird? home for me? "

    Swallow, you really perverse little Swallow!
    South, it was south that I wanted to follow!
    But *there* you go fluttering, mile after mile,
    East into Egypt—east to the Nile!

    Being so proud that a Pyramid's hollow!
    Oh what an archæological Swallow!
    You could have skimmed through a Calabar hut—
    Yet you aren't doing it—anything *but !*

You could have said that from June to December,
Winter to summer, I *always* remember!
You could have perched on a palm-tree above—
Given my love to them—given my love!

The Nun :

Dear little Feather-Thoughts, to and fro flying—
Surely my Feather-Thoughts won't begin cry-
ing?
Out from the Ark you have travelled, my Dove:
Given His love to them—given His love.

SUMS

LITTLE Veronica sat on her chair,
　Nibbled her pencil and nibbled her hair!
Wished she was anywhere, anywhere, *anywhere*—
　Only not *there* !
Doing her sums on a slippery chair!

Little Veronica looked at the clock.
" Tickety, tickety, tickety tock! "
Mopped up a tear with the edge of her frock—
　O what a clock!
Couldn't it hurry its tickety-tock?

Little Veronica heaved . . . great . . . sighs.
Little Veronica shut . . . both . . . eyes . . .
(When you are dozy-ing, how the time flies!—
　And, what a surprise!
Can they be—can they be—Calabar skies?)

　Sister Veronica squats on the sand.
　Black-a-black babies have hold of her hand.
　Hark at them wanting to understand!
　　Isn't it grand?
　Learning arithmetic out in the sand!

　But Sister Veronica couldn't do sums.
　Multiplication?　Her little head hums!

"If one loaf is sixpence, how much are the
    crumbs?"
  Fingers and thumbs!
The more she goes counting, the wronger it
    comes!

"Sister Veronica, please don't cry!"
(Little black fingers the tear-drops dry.)
"Sister Veronica—don't you try—
  We'll-show-you-how-to-do-it !
Then you can manage it, by-and-by!"

Little Veronica woke with a jump,
Home from West Africa thumpety-thump.
There she was sitting, a little pink lump,
  Ever so plump,
Safe in the old mathematical clump!

Little Veronica thought: "Oh dear!
How very happy I am to be here!
Start again! Two-and-two wouldn't appear
  To-make-five-but-then-Oh-dear-what-DO-they-
    make?"
Work at it, darling, there's nothing to fear!

XII

BLESSED MARTIN PORRES, O.P.;
a Black Saint, Patron of Rats.

O Lord—
I am a Black!
  They don't think much of *that*!
  Less than they think of a Rat . . .
O Lord—
  Your Black *feels* like a Rat!

O Lord—
I am so small!
  And they, so white and tall!
  Why worry for me at all?
O Lord—
  Why *should* they?

O Lord—
I did what I could
For your little Rats;
  And they said: " That's
  All you are good for! "
O Lord—
  They were perfectly right.

Lord—
That's all I was good for.
  Yet wasn't I proud
  That You allowed

Me to do something for those
Who were hunted, God knows . . .
   Hunted . . .
As You and Your Mother were.

Ah, Love,
   Can it be
   That in the way *You* see
I am white after all?
   In Your marvellous sight,
   After all, am I white?
Yes, I am; for Your red
Blood that was shed
   Washes me, washes me White.

Ah, Black, Red, White!
   Sin, Sacrifice, Salvation!
   What matter my nation?
My colour? my speech?
For all and for each
   You opened Your Heart.
   And I, for my part,
Creep into Your Love—my Darling—my Dove!
   What joy shall I lack?
   I the Rat?   I the Black?
Through the dead black, the cold grey,
   Gleams Gold!

XIII

THE BOY IN THE MIDST OF THEM

SAINT MARTHA, as you might expect, was in
the kitchen cooking:
So Sara, as she often did, when Martha wasn't
looking,
Crept off to Auntie Mary who was sitting by the
trees,
And Auntie Mary took her up and put her on her
knees.

Now Auntie Mary always knew when things were
not quite right,
And so she didn't say a word but hugged her baby
tight.
At last: " I've been so naughty," little Sara said,
" to-day;
When nobody was looking, I got up and ran away!

For that was just the very time, I'd heard the people
tell,
When Jesus goes and sits among the children by
the well.
And when He saw me coming—oh! He looked at
me and smiled,
And said: ' To-night I want to talk about a little
child!

So I shall pick out one of you for everyone to see . . .'
Oh Auntie! *wouldn't* you have thought He meant
to pick out *me ?*
But just when I was running out and simply wild
with joy—
What *do* you think? He went and chose a *horrid
little boy !* "

Saint Mary kissed her tears away and said: " My
darling dear,
This very night He's promised us to come to supper
here!
And so, for once, I really think that you can sit up
late,
And bring His bread, and bring His grapes, and
put them on His plate! "

O broken Bread! O Wine-drops shed! O Gift
beyond all price!
A little child is told to lift the ancient Sacrifice!
What you in Him, O Seraphim, immortally adore
A child of days is bidden raise—You could not
offer more!

And after supper Jesus put His Sara on His knee,
And once again He said: " But let My baby come
to Me! "

31

He thanked her for her kindness, and He kissed her
   sleepy head,
And then He came with *both* her Aunts, and tucked
   her up in bed.

XIV

OUR LADY IMMACULATE,
LIMEHOUSE

" Upon the Bells . . . ' Holiness to the Lord.' "
Zach. xiv. 20.

A.D. 0

Drift, dim River, down to the empty Sea:
  Wash, waste waters, over the misty fen:
Scarcely a cry of bird, and never a taller tree—
  Never a footfall faint, and never the noise of men!

A.D. 1000

Dance, strong stream, 'twixt hazel and scented lime!
  Float, white sails; then turn to your hamlet home!
Drift, soft smoke; and tinkle, O chapel chime;
  Answer the sacring-bells that sweet from the
    westward come!

A.D. 1600

Splash, splendid Thames! To Greenwich a
    gorgeous Queen
  Rows superb, and proudly her concert swells!
Sound, bugles, sound! But over the meadows
    green
  No wind more wafts music of sacring-bells.

A.D. 1859

Gnaw, foul flood, your filthy and festering flanks!
  Smear, poisoned swirl, the murderous Limehouse
    shore!
Ah—but hark! from over the brutal banks
  Hark what tells that Christ is alive once more!

A.D. 1939

Chime, brave Carillon, clear above speed and spate!
  Shine, Sacred Heart, far over the waters grey!
Gleam, White Mary, Our Lady Immaculate
  Pray — for — Limehouse — Immaculate Mary,
    pray!

Limehouse was a distant hamlet getting its name either from lime-kilns or from lime-trees. The history of both, in England, is very old, and both derivations are credible. Bells, too, existed much earlier than we here picture them as doing; and, in a fair wind, nothing will have prevented Limehouse from hearing the bells of St. Peter's abbey at Westminster. —Only in the eighteenth and nineteenth centuries did Limehouse acquire its appalling reputation. Already it is much transformed: even 'Chinatown', in the old sense, is no more. And the parish is much developed. It was the saintly Fr. F. H. Higley, whose rectorship began in 1888, who determined on the stately church that now faces the Commercial Rd., with its campanile and carillon, its stature of Mary Immaculate and that of the Sacred Heart overlooking the Thames that has undergone such strange vicissitudes.

CORPUS CHRISTI, MAIDEN LANE, W.C.2

" And He was made Flesh of the Maiden Mary : and He was made Man." The Creed.

FAR back in brown Australia I'd heard about the Strand—
A golden street—a palace-street—with Dukes on every hand!
I'd made a bit of money, so I said I'd go and see,
And spend a flamin' fortnight in the lap o' luxury!

I have to own, that narrow street upset me quite a bit;
And how they told such tales of it surpasses human wit.
And lonely? nothing lonelier save when you might be canned,
Than an Aussie, knowing no one, in a Palace by the Strand.

One summer day, I lost meself, and down it come to rain,
And quite by chance I struck a street entitled Maiden Lane.
I bolted for a porch—and if it didn't beat the band!
It was a church, a Catholic church, quite close behind the Strand!

The Church was ' Corpus Christi ', and ' Maiden
　　Lane ' the street—
O Blessed Virgin, 'twasn't you I had the right to
　　meet.
Yet, Lady, greater lady than the greatest in the land,
Thank God I should have met you here, so neigh-
　　bour to the Strand!

The church was sweet with roses out of Covent
　　Garden come:
And Jesus Christ was there Himself to make me feel
　　at home.
O 'Christ, a Man the same as me, I knew you'd
　　understand
What fills the silly heads of them that's drifting
　　down the Strand!

In comes a priest. I polish up. I goes to Mass
　　next day
And makes my good Communion, and awestruck
　　slips away.
And how I blessed—oh *how* I blessed—the heavenly
　　thought that planned
That most mysterious little church that waits behind
　　the Strand!

WESTMINSTER CATHEDRAL

(They all kneel where they can see the great Crucifix hanging high.)
" I, if I be lifted up, will draw all men to Myself."
Jn. xii. 32

I. The Child

When I am taken for a walk
  My nurse must often do some shopping;
And if she doesn't want to talk
  She says: " No harm about your stopping
    In the Cathedral for a bit!
    I know how fond you are of it! "

Of course I know it's holy ground,
  So down I kneel in adoration.
But then I like to wander round
  And do a little exploration.
    Well, it's a sort of holy fun
    Discovering what's being done!

I like St. Andrew's chapel best
  With golden fans upon the ceiling:
He travelled east—he travelled west—
  I spell the cities while I'm kneeling.
    But when he'd done with ships and wrecks
    He died upon a wooden X!

And then, from time to time I start
    To save up sweets or else a penny,
And cross to You, dear Sacred Heart,
    To see if someone hasn't any.
        For *there*, one easily might meet
        A child that's not enough to eat!

Then I look up to Jesus Christ
    Throned on His heavenly Cross above me,
And think how much *He* sacrificed
    To show how dearly He did love me.
        I was a very happy child
        When Jesus Christ looked down and smiled.

II. The Nun (*opposite the Chapel of the Blessed
Sacrament*)

Must it then be a life of naught but ' No '?
Not music is God's voice; nor sunset glow
    For me may be His glory?   Never for me
    The hills, the moor, the sea?

And must I have no friend of friends to love?
Must all my poor experiments but prove
    That sole renunciation is the road
    By which I must have trod?

Dear fainting spirit!   Freely here express
How long may seem your hour of loneliness!
    Unseen, unguessed, in its small shrine apart,
    Lives the Most Sacred Heart!

If, lifted at your long procession's head,
The Crucifix must preach you Jesus Dead—
    Never a day there was, but with you went
    The Blessed Sacrament.

III. The Working-Man (near The Chapel of Our Lady)

WHEN forth to work I fare each day
        I can't give much beyond a minute.
But the Cathedral's on my way;
    And so I pass those moments in it.

I tip-toe down the right-hand aisle,
    And there with anxious thoughts I grapple,
Hoping to catch St. Joseph's smile,
    And Mary's from her silver chapel.

Or else I turn my looks up high,
    And watch the Crucifix above me;
For me You didn't doubt to die,
    It's good to think that You approve me!

And when the day seems very long,
　　When spirits sink and hopes are coldest,
And when the whole round world goes wrong,
　　And life might terrify the boldest—

And when I fear to lose my job
　　And don't see how to find another,
And haven't got an extra bob
　　To give a treat to Dad and Mother—

And think how Peggy's got to slave
　　To keep the children as they should be—
And if the world weren't fool or knave
　　How very different things *could* be—

Ah, well!　Thy hands were pretty rough;
　　Thy Heart was heavier than mine is—
And I shall think it good enough
　　If mine is half as brave as Thine is.

So, when it's time for turning home,
　　Whatever be the thing that ails me—
Back, great Cathedral, back I come
　　To thank the One who never fails me.

*IV. The Unbeliever (by the Chapel of the Souls in
Purgatory)*

O God . . .
    That wasn't a prayer, for I
  Cannot believe in a God. So it was
Some sort, I suppose, of a sigh—
Disgust, or fatigue, or because
I'm sick of it all.   That's why
  I sit here so often, and stare,
  And breathe this exempted air.

That is it!   Exempted.   This place
Gives me a breathing-space
  In the horrible labour of living;
A reprieve from the having to cope
  With that obstinate unforgiving
Pest, that is human hope . . .
  From all of the dreams that I dreamt
  As a boy, in *here* I'm exempt.

Perhaps I'm a coward to sneak
  In here, like so many I know—
But we never would notice, nor speak
  To each other about it, but go
Back separate, into routine,
Work, apathy, pleasure, venality;
Too shy to admit we have been
  In here, to escape from reality . . .

Yes, Christ, if You only were real,
    I'd have what I'm needing, a plan
For my life, and a goal, and not feel
    What a meaningless creature is Man.
They vouch that Your anguish immense
    Can *save*.   I'd gladly endure
Any Cross, if it only made sense—
    If it left me a little more pure!
You challenging Church!   What am I
    To become, in your difficult air?
What else can I answer, but cry—
    " O God—if that *might* be a prayer? "

XVII

ST. ALOYSIUS: SOMERS TOWN

" The Lord maketh the Seeing Eye."—Prov. xx. 12.

DUKES went walking in Clarendon Square,
　Snuffing its highly salubrious air.
Wasn't it grand to be noticed there,
In aristocratical Clarendon Square?

But Clarendon Square came down with a bump.
Dukes were the first to be 'ware of the slump:
Dowagers vowed that the place was a frump:
Baronets bellowed it gave 'em the hump!

But Frenchmen had built them a church hard by.
Over the Altar a gilded Eye
Watched each worshipper sleeplessly—
And saw how a skivvy came there to cry.

　　" Clarendon Square! Clarendon Square!
　　Couldn't I cry my heart out there!
　　Dark in a corner I'd make my prayer—
　　No one to bully me; none to stare! "

At first she was rather afraid of the Eye
Gazing at *her* so steadfastly . . .
But soon—she couldn't have told you why—
She found she had frankly forgotten to cry.

The Presence of God enfolded her quite:
When forth she went, the slums turned bright:
Through rain and fogs she walked in His Light—
Glad she should never be out of His sight!

Far must she travel from Clarendon Square;
Heavier burdens the Servant must bear.
But ever her myriad children share
In the Grace that streamed from Clarendon Square.

XVIII

THE ORATORY

"My House shall be called a House of Prayer."—Matt. xxi. 13.

"PRAY—pray—pray—pray!"
　　Hear the Oratory say!

Hither turn your flagging feet
From the hot and hunted street.
If it's simply tired you are—
Should you feel that Heaven's far—
Out from glare and into gloom,
Come and pray—there's always room!

Should you be guilty, still come in:
Heave from your heart the load of sin.
I think your soul would feel at home
Underneath my dusky domè.

Here can the shrivelled spirit borrow
Tears from Our Lady and her sorrow:
Here finds the bruisèd brain relief
When bowed before th' Apostles' Chief.
Here rest, disheartened one, awhile
'Neath Philip's kind courageous smile!

45

Pray—pray—pray—pray!
And if you can't find words to say
Why should you trouble? Cannot He
Explore your soul's intricacy?
When you are dead—when you are dumb—
Will not the Holy Spirit come
And deep within your prayerless mood
Pray as you never did nor could?
(And He who knows man's Innermost
Shall listen to His Holy Ghost.)

And if you are but lonely—see!
We have a " Little Orat'ry "!
Come and make friends—for here are they
Who'll welcome you, and also pray!
And friendship is a pearl unpriced
When, for a third, your friend is Christ.
So what *could* Oratorians say
Save " Pray, my friend and Brother—pray! "

XIX

WELWYN GARDEN CITY:
ST. BONAVENTURE'S

THE gallant knights of olden days—
 Went spurring forth on difficult ways.
O Brave Adventure, should they see—
Some maiden tethered to a tree!
The dreadful Dragon, snorting flame
Went white as ashes when they came.
The Brigand Baron, in his tower,
Did when he spied them, cringe and cower.
  A Good Adventure, you'll agree!—
  But where is now our Chivalrie?

Well, there be those who swear, to-day,
With slimy slum to make away.
They'll build a Garden City—wise
And kindly-hearted enterprise!
Let " rose, carnation, lily, rose "
Bedeck the bijou bungalows!
Let Homesteads (mildly modernist)
Blush, by Virginia's creeper kissed!
  But then, you can't (distressful fact)
  Keep *any* Paradise intact!

For see!   Beyond the puffing train
Lord Industry begins again.
Where silver birches idly stood
Are wafted whiffs from Hollywood.

Practical houses, squarely planned,
By solid streets symmetric stand.
Admire our workmen's Uplift Clubs!
Esteem our sleek hygienic Pubs!
    Sir, and/or Madam, pray advance
    Our Venture of such high Finance!

Saint Bonaventure! Were not you
The least bit startled by that view?
Did you expect your open field
Would quite that sort of harvest yield?
Best of Adventurers! Your aid
We beg for this our new Crusade!
Undaunted, we your succour ask
In this our hard and heavenly task.
    There may we plant unfading flowers—
    There build the Eternal City's towers!

XX

QUO VADITIS?

For the Flock House Emigrant Boys : 1928

QUEEN ELIZABETH sat one day,
  Watching the Tilbury guns at play;
With Walter Raleigh bold and gay
  And Drake the red Sea-Rover.
' 'Pon my soul ', said great Queen Bess,
' These are the pick of the lads, I guess:
' I couldn't say more, and I mustn't say less—
  ' They're known the whole world over! '

Suddenly out of the sea so green
Father Neptune's head was seen.
' Pardon me, Madam ', said he to the Queen,
  ' Pardon me, red Sea-Rover.
' Certainly I admire your grit;
' Still I suggest you should wait a bit.
' I've plenty of lads that shall equal it
  ' From Dundee down to Dover.'

' Quite impossible, sir,' she said:
' Chase such notions out of your head.
' Swim away home and go to bed '
  (And so said Drake the Rover).

49

' These are the boys that have swept the seas,
' Baffled the brisk Atlantic breeze.
' Even America's heard of these,
    ' And so has Terra Nova.'

' All very well ', said the god of the sea;
' No one's denying it, good Queen B.;
' But some of the lads I have got with me
    ' Go twice as far from Dover.
' Panama's only a half of the way
' They shall go travelling one fine day.
' What'll you answer to that, I pray?
    ' You and your red Sea-Rover? '

Queen Elizabeth shook her head:
' Shakespeare tells the tale ', she said:
' But never I've heard and never I've read
    ' Romancers such as *you* are! '
' Come, Your Majesty, yield to fate!
' I'll tell you the ship and I'll tell you the date:
' It's nineteen hundred and twenty-eight—
    ' The ship's the *Rotorua*.

' And as for the lads, I think,' said he,
' You can be proud of 'em same as me—
' Sailing across the distant sea,
    ' Sailing away from Dover.

'Sailing away to the golden West,
'Each of them anxious to do his best;
'Working and playing with zeal and zest
  'Till work and play are over.'

(With further apologies to
the *Harrow Song Book*.)

XXI

"HERE, SIR!"

LONG ago, they tell the story,
    Lads would sail to lands afar,
Seeking gold or seeking glory,
    Each believing in his star—
East or West—Scorning rest—
    Pole, Peru, or Malabar.
Here, Sir! here, Sir! here, Sir! here Sir! (*spoken*)
    When they heard the distant call—
Here, Sir! here, Sir! here, Sir! here, Sir! (*spoken*)
    They'd be present, one and all.

Still to-day from smoke and city,
    Still to-day from field and farm,
Asking neither plaint nor pity,
    Beating back each base alarm—
Man or lad—grave or glad—
    Ships and sails without alarm.
Here, Sir! here, Sir! here, Sir! here, Sir! (*spoken*)
    When they hear the distant call—
Here, Sir! here, Sir! here, Sir! here, Sir! (*spoken*)
    See them present, one and all.

Still, persuade us, please, New Zealand,
    Once we mix your men among
High though be our hopes when *we* land,
    We shall still be fairly young!

You must teach—All and each—
  How to work and hold their tongue.
Here, Sir! here, Sir! here, Sir! here, Sir! (*spoken*)
  Be the motto boldly sung!
Here, Sir! here, Sir! here, Sir! here, Sir! (*spoken*)
  Learn the job, and hold your tongue!

Mind and muscle duly strengthened,
  Men of brawn and men of brain,
Send us out with stirrup lengthened,
  Out with flock and out for grain.
Scythe and shear—Cloud or clear—
  Horse and dog and sheep and grain!
Here, Sir! here, Sir! here, Sir! here, Sir! (*spoken*)
  Tough the task and stiff the strain!
Here, Sir! here, Sir! here, Sir! here, Sir! (*spoken*)
  Do the work and start again!

When the tale of toil is finished,
  When the final count is near,
Then, with courage undiminished
  Face the future without fear!
Comes the call—One and all—
  May we answer: ' We are here! "
Here, Sir! here, Sir! here, Sir! here, Sir! (*spoken*)
  Answer swift the urgent cry—
Here, Sir! here, Sir! here, Sir! here, Sir! (*spoken*)
  Faithful hearts shall never die!

                    (With further apologies to
                    the *Harrow Song Book*.)

E   53

XXII

SEAMAN BOUND FOR HEAVEN

"COULD you," said he, "stop on a bit? I heard
the nurses say
I'm due for packing up—maybe to-morrow or next
day."
I said: "Of course I'll stop, and come to-morrow
too, don't fear."
He said: "You mustn't trouble—'cos you mightn't
find me here."

He said: "It's quite a distance out from London
to the Dock!"
I said: "Don't be so silly—fifty minutes by the
clock!
What's that, compared with you, that's travelled
half your life on sea?"
"Four year!" he smiled: "*That* ain't the half! I'm
all of twenty-three!

"Four year of doing everything I didn't should 'ave
done;
Four year, committing every sin that's underneath
the sun!
Four year, that I have trodden every step that led
to 'ell . . ."
"But then," said I, "you must have done some
heavenly things as well?"

" When I was in Australia—well, I saw a thing or
        two . . ."
And then he rambled off about the skies of ardent
        blue,
The misty gold of wattle, and the Sydney Bridge,
        and trees
So silver-straight beneath the moon, a-shiver in the
        breeze.

*O hungry eyes, that starved upon the devil's
        hideousness—*
Yet saw so much to feed on in God-given loveliness !
O may this oil absolve you, and His *loving-
        kindliness*
*Whose Eyes can see, and understand, our human
        faultiness !*

" When down at Durban," so he said, " I listened
        to a song
That roars within my wretched ears half day and
        all night long.
And yet, would you believe it, when them Zulus
        started in,
I heard a sound within my soul that made me loathe
        to sin . . ."

O then, if they *had mysteries to whisper to thy mind,*
What shall not He *impart to thee, so infinitely
        kind ?*

55

*Ah, Voice beneath all voices—oh, Spirit softly
    crying—*
*Anoint his ears—he hears ! he hears, for whom all
    sounds are dying !*

" But Father, you would not believe the words that
        I let rip . . .
Why, even now they're trembling-like upon my
        very lip.
Yet never was a night but what ' Hail Mary ' would
        I say,
Save when I might be too ashamed, and same at
        break of day."

*Ah, human voice, uplifted in man's anguish to
    blaspheme—*
*Ah, Mary, shining white across the darkest human
    dream !*
*Ah, Cross of Christ—ah, kiss of Christ on lips so
    nearly dumb—*
*Your boy is off to silence—let him hear You bid him
    ' come ' !*

" Now, Father, what my hands have done and where
        my feet have bore—"
" Hush, hush, my son; I know it all—Port Said to
        Singapore . . .

But then, your mate he told me how, near Aden,
    in the dark,
You jumped off ship to save a man, and never
    thought of shark,

" And never stayed to wonder if he mightn't pull
    you down,
Might pull you after him, dear Jack—might pull
    you in to drown! "
    (O feet that sped—O hands that clutched—O flesh
    that might have bled !
    O friend, to friend so true, that you would even die
    instead !)

    Most holy all-absolving oil ! O wisest tenderness
    Of God all-pitying, will not You absolve and richly
    bless
    These hands and feet that worked and walked so
    very far from Thee—
    This heart, wherein was greater love than other love
    could be ?

" I ain't got nothing; " he went on: " this very
    shirt ain't mine . . ."
    (O soul, O body, wrapped around in marriage-dress
    divine !)
" I'm dying destitute," said he: " I ain't got naught
    but Christ . . ."
    (Well, wasn't He for thee—for thee—the wholly
    Sacrificed ?)

O Lord, this man, just setting forth upon the final
    sea—
How should not he, Thou Pilot, come to shore, to
    home, with Thee ?
Has he indeed no thing at all—no journey-money
    even ?
But how shouldst Thou not lift him now, Thou
    Welcome, into heaven !

Thyself his great Viaticum, Thyself his Guarantee ;
Thy Name upon his sailor's book inscribed for all to
    see !
Thy son—and mine—acknowledged now our own,
    our very own—
How could you dream that you should die, dear
    Jackie, all alone ?

THE CUP

WE recently received a letter from Salt Lake Ranch, Refugio, Texas, and on the ranch is a tiny chapel, Our Lady Star of the Sea, by a little bay running into the Gulf of Mexico. The place is called Lamar and was once flourishing, but has been almost wiped out since it was sacked by the Union troops during the Civil War. Till the present road was put through, the only method of approach was by water over a shallow reefy bay. The chapel was built of burnt oyster-shells and has a congregation varying from 3 to 14—one or two nearby residents and others who propose to spend the day fishing or shooting. Our correspondent's wife (he is a convert cattle-raiser) remembers the chapel when it was derelict. One of her aunts discovered it, weed-grown and inhabited by owls. In a mouldering chest were the priest's vestments, rotten with sea air and damp; and standing on the altar was the Chalice . . . Why did they leave it there? Who knows? Anyhow, there it remained until our own time, and the chapel is reconsecrated.

CHRIST'S CUP

BESIDE the Gulf of Mexico,
Three times a hundred years ago

The townlet called Lamar
Did vow to build a seaside shrine
For her, whose care is yours and mine—
  For Mary, Seamen's Star.
They built the church of oyster-shells;
And sweet the chime of silver bells,
From market-place to convent-cells
  Made music near and far.

And lads and lasses trooped to pray,
On many a distant yesterday—
  A gladdening sight to scan!
But came a harsh and heathen hour:
Men sacked the town and took the tower—
  Disgrace to God and man!
They stole the silver, burned the wood;
Made mock of Mary, smashed the Rood—
Yet left the Chalice where it stood—
  Explain it, if you can!

Poor empty Cup, that opens wide
The mouth wherein God's blood has dried
  Which flowed to save my soul:
The starry skies are roofed with night:
The altar-candles quenchèd quite,
  And dead the censer's coal.
And spider, scorpion, bats and owl
And all the fateful things and foul
That wake at midnight, come to prowl
  And peer within your bowl.

Christ, fasting in the wilderness,
The wild beasts asked Thee them to bless—
　　Not one didst Thou disdain!
They gave Thee welcome, in their way;
They felt You'd come another day—
　　" Dear Christ, You'll come again?
Oh, Christ, a hateful beast am I—
Deserve my hell eternally—
But why did You consent to die,
　　If *not* to snap my chain? "

Rejoice, rejoice, you empty Cup!
Once more He comes to fill you up!
　　How *could* He say you Nay?
For Christ is risen from the dead—
Once more the snowy cloths are spread—
　　New sunlight gilds the grey!
O Bells, no more be dead, be dumb!
O Bread, He consecrates each crumb!
O Vine, your sacring hour is come!
　　The Lord is here to stay!

XXIV

SEAMAN'S HOSPITAL CLOCK

TICK TOCK ! Hospital Clock—
You did a good deed to-day !
" Pooh, pooh ! How could I do
Anything out of the way ? "

Listen to me, you obstinate Clock !
Nobody needs to do
Extra things—astonishing things—
But simply their job, like you !

Young Jimmy he lay with his broken back, and
wished that the day were done,
He couldn't get out, as the others had got, out to
the afternoon sun.
Young Jimmy was brave, but a man's heart sinks
when Time goes pitiless by;
Young Jimmy began to ask himself if possibly he
would die.
You mustn't rebuke him, for thoughts go crook
when a man is as lonely as he;
His world turned black—when suddenly, Clock,
when suddenly *you struck Three !*
Young Jimmy, his hand went up to his brow, and
he drew it across his breast,
And he started to say: " In the Name of the
Father——" (you certainly know the rest).

Young Jimmy pulled up with a bit of a jerk. He
    hadn't done that, thought he,
For many a year—not blessed himself (let alone
    when a Clock struck Three) . . .
But distant dreams of his school in the Bush came
    flickering into his head—
The Brothers, they hadn't knocked much into *that*,
    but hammered his knuckles instead!
One Brother was rough, and another was stiff, and
    another was easy and kind—
Jim thought it was queer that for such a long time
    they hadn't come into his mind.
He thought of the smell of the gums, and the ink,
    of the Chapel (he shivered)—and see!
They had taught him to make the sign of the Cross
    at Twelve and again at Three.
Well, at twelve in the ward there was plenty of
    noise; and, Clock, if he listened to *you*,
The only thought that'd come to his head was,
    Dinner is almost due.
At three he was probably fast asleep—but, who can
    tell why? to-day
He was fairly awake, and for once he heard the
    message you had to say:

" He too—He too—was nailed to a cruel bed:
  He too—like you—though His was a Cross
    instead.

She too—she too—Mary was there at Three;
  She too—she too—had counted the hours, like
  me."

Well, all I can add, you inquisitive Clock, is this—
  When I came that night,
Young Jimmy declared with the ghost of a grin,
  that he wanted to put things right.
He pulled out his hand, and the Cross he'd begun
  he finished from brow to breast—
From shoulder to shoulder, and started at once:
  " I confess . . ." (but you know the rest).

  *So, tick, tock, friendly old Clock—What have you
  got to say ?*
  *" Tick, tock," answered the Clock, " I'm grateful to
  God to-day——"*
  *Solemnly answered the Hospital Clock—" God has
  been good to-day."*

XXV

PRAISE HIM, FIRE AND ICE! PRAISE HIM, HILLS AND SEA!

Summer in New Zealand : A Mass at Waihi.
" Feed Thou upon the Heart of the Stranger."
(A Maori Offering.)

WHEN north we drove from Wellington—
    July! July!
The air was silver-golden—
    An emerald sky!
And orange flared the willow-twigs against the
    blackened yews,
And all horizons melted in an ecstasy of blues.

When down we dropped to Taupo—
    The fire! the snow!
Ngáuruhóë fulminant;
    The lake below.
A night of frozen shadows, till with a shout the Sun
Leapt, and the steam went swirling to salute the
    Day begun.

Then down the mountain Mass-ward—
    Intent they stood,
Brown Maoris round the Altar,
    Unshod, tattooed.

65

O Christ, speed swift across the snows; float firm
across the flood!
I offer for New Zealand Thy pure, Thy fiery Blood!

Christmas in London : A Mass at Farm Street.
Ana to kai na : " Behold thy Food."

When Christmas came to England—
The rain! the grey!
How might you think that visitors
Should come? should stay?
Yet sinewy New Zealanders (All Black, though
shriven white . . .)
Tramped up to their Communion through the
heart of Christmas night.

For even in our England—
Noël! Noël!—
'Mid mistletoe and holly,
The Bell! the Bell!
Not here the red pohuta nor the huia plume—but
then
The self-same Shepherd folded in unbarriered
Bethlehem.

Christmas in Perth, W. Australia ; 1928

When midnight *Missa Est* was sung; I climbed my
terrace-bed;
The blue Australian starlight signed its Crosses on
my head.

O Dawn, be distant! stars, be slow—the days have
   grown so few
Before I sail for England and must say Good-bye
   to you.
Yet, Dawn, it's you that light the crocus-flame on
   Christmas trees;
Unveil the red volcanic eucalyptus; bring the
   breeze
That swings the surf to smother all the beach—and
   doubtless I
Had better see all this once more, though but to say
   Good-bye.

*Christmas ; Perth ; 1934. In memory of
   Archbishop Clune*

Another Christmas I was there,
   And round the Terrace sighing,
Adeste filled the midnight air,
   For you, dear friend, lay dying:
Your creamy-grey Cathedral down below
Relayed to you its ' Come ye! ' Be it so.

Black ruffled Swan, go call God's Dove,
   And sweeten your keen crying:
The old Archbishop whom I love
   Lies under me a-dying.
Why must Australia always make me mix
So much of joy with so much crucifix?

And I shall leave before the end—
    They call it ' end '—befalls him:
Nor shall I heavenward help to send
    Him when the New Year calls him.
Well, Memory, that have so much to do!
Here's one more not too difficult task for
    you.

Australian English Summers : Cricket and Coronation

When summer came to London Town
    You too were there!
So glad was I, I couldn't care
Which way the Ashes went or where—
    You came to London Town.
You upon Poplar roofs your ball
Bowled, and they hit it one and all,
And bowled *you* out—the Lord knows how—
The night was pleasant, you'll allow!
And if I thought the plushy swards
And all the elegance of Lord's
Couldn't compare with Poplar brick—
Well, cricket's somehow Catholic:
I'd like to think that our ' Well Come! '
Made you feel almost-half-at-home:
And when we said our Goodnight prayer,
    You too were there.

Well, if I'm never more to see
The land that grew so dear to me,
Nor any more watch Aden sink
Sun-bleached beneath the fateful brink;
Nor, between blues of butterflies,
Dream—Which are seas? and which are skies?
Nor turn from silvery Brisbane back
And beg the shelter of some shack
And hear the petulant pepper-trees
Rattle their berries in the breeze,
Nor wonder, less than half awake,
If palm-tree rustle means a snake—
Nor, beneath Sydney Bridge, my cap
Doff, nor admire your offered Gap . . .
Nor stormily from Melbourne drive
And come to Ballarat alive,
Nor swallow all that desert-dust,
Taking my destiny on trust;
Nor into Adelaide come down—
Blue-purple, crimson-golden town—
    Snapdragons and geraniums,
    Rose, larkspur and delphiniums . . .
Nor back again to Goodbye-Perth
Over those leagues of rusted earth—
Worst, if I'll no more recognise
Such welcome in your laughing eyes,
Dear soldiers of so long ago—
Well, still you're there, and still I know

That both in Bush and City I
Would friendship find that doesn't die.
   O heart, not older grow nor grey!
   Treasure your every yesterday!
   Cross, rooted deep in earth I trod—
   Cross, you whose summit touches God—
   Cross, stretch your two arms out so wide
   That not one man be left outside!
   And if, poor heart, you homesick feel,
   Kneel, little life, contented kneel!
   Fade, Europe! fade, Australia!
   Our home is fixed *in patria*!

XXVI

TRANSFIGURATION

(NIGHT. The open Sea. Choppy weather. In spite of the dark, you see ridges of white surf appearing and disappearing. There is sufficient mist just to make the sky indistinguishable from the water. The water is always there, swaying enormously without any true advance. It has therefore its vast but almost inert consciousness; whereas the waves are each of them new, momentarily aware, but without experience. They break into a million drops of spray, but even the spray has no time to learn anything. A Sea-Bird, swept out by some gale and now exhausted, flies darkly over the water, trying to settle on it from time to time, to rest; but it immediately rises again, having lost the control of its instinct, and knowing itself doomed.)

THE SEA-BIRD: Nothing, nothing, nothing!

(The Sea admits that the Bird is there, but does nothing for it, and says nothing to it.)

THE WAVES: I begin! I heave myself! I race, and with a million hands! I . . . (*they scatter into surf*).

THE SURF: Whither? whither? whither? (*It vanishes.*)

THE BIRD: I cannot, I cannot, I cannot! No rock; no turfy rock; no more any nest. . . . Nothing,

nothing, nothing. (*It subsides on the water with outspread wings, its eyes staring but glazed. It surrenders.*)

THE SPRAY: I drench it—I rain rapidly upon it.

THE WAVES: What is this upon me? I will not have it. I——

(The Sea smothers it and there is no more Bird.)

THE SPRAY: Where is it? what was it?

THE WAVES: Was there something?

(For a while the Sea continues to move in an immense and meaningless tumult. The Waves have their brief moment of expectation, and indignant check, while the Spray flies to and fro, and half of it is whirled into the air and joins the mist, while the rest relapses into the Waves which do not recognize it.

Looking Westward, you see an emerald light, and a ruby light, both dimmed by distance and mist, and, high above them, a white light, dimmer still. They heave and dip, for the Ship that carries them is pitching violently. At last you see the Ship, a towering black mass, blacker than the Sea or the Sky. As it proceeds, it cuts the wind that is pouring against it into two, and the Wind streams with intense anger to this side and that, tossed to and fro by the currents of air making eddies and exasperation overhead and to right and left. As for the Water, it gets forced no less violently to either side, in great curves mounting into surf of their

72

own. They rush outwards and encounter the normal Surf and conflict hissingly with it. For a while the Surf made by the Ship runs forward above the Waves and their Spray; but soon enough it gets pounded underneath, and, were it daylight, you could see it struggling and gasping under the surface, till it gives up, and clouds away like a soul dissolving under your very eyes.)

THE SHIP (*trembling to the rhythm of its Engines*): I'm bound to go on. Bound to go on. It's difficult, but I'm bound to go on. It's difficult, difficult, difficult.

THE ENGINES: *We* don't care! We don't care! We don't care!

(Their glistening masses of steel swing round and their shafts slide to and fro in the most perfect accuracy, impassive, not even obediently after all.)

THE SHIP: I'm bound to go on.

THE SEA (*suddenly alert and indignant*): Why?

THE SHIP: It's got to be done. There isn't a Why. I know nothing of Why.

THE ENGINES: We make you; we make you!

THE SEA: But why? (*The Engines pay no attention whatsoever.*)

(The Water under the Ship finds itself suddenly sucked swiftly up through a pipe; it encounters a mass of cinders and ashes and spouts forward carrying them with it; the Water and the Ashes are ejected in a filthy stream from the side of the Ship. The down-ward arc of water flies through the air in unspeak-able indignation till abruptly it re-encounters the Sea, and the whole is absorbed and in a moment is drowned into forgetfulness of this event. Similarly the Air is suddenly seized upon and dragged down-wards, too astonished so much as to protest, and cannonaded through a ventilating-shaft into the Stoke-Hole, where it instantly gets full of grit and black dust, of which it drops as much as it can before being whirled up again and vanishing who knows whither, filthied at first, but almost imme-diately cleaned, like the Water, in its own element.

The Sea with inarticulate rage tries to beat back the Surf driving into it from the Ship.)

THE WAVES AND THEIR SPRAY: What are you at? This is not your way! Do not come this way. You are attacking us . . . Surf! What can you mean by it? You are our self! You must not attack us.

THE SHIP'S SURF: I cannot help it. I don't mean to attack you. How can I help it? I am driven.

THE SEA'S SPRAY (*breaking into innumerable tears*): Surf, you are stifling me! Surf, do not run over me like that!

THE SHIP'S SURF (*heaving itself outward more obstinately and violently than ever.*) I tell you I can't help it. Get out of my way. If I drown you, it isn't my fault.

THE WAVES: Oh, it isn't, isn't it? You *would*, would you? Take that, then! (*The outward-rushing surge has reached the point where the Wave can heave itself up and submerge it.*)

THE SHIP'S SURF (*hissing as it expires*): Surf of the Sea, you slay me, you sink me! I was—It wasn't my fault. . . .

(The Surf is submerged, and the Waves clap themselves flat and hard against the Ship's sides, but in a moment, new Surf is thrown outwards, and the Waves lie backwards, swim away, and begin their assault once more, just as uselessly.)

THE SEA (*entering into gigantic communion with the Air*): Air! When you weigh heavily upon me all the day and the night, that is not conflict! Even when you stir me into waves, I am not suffering!

THE AIR: Sea, you are cruelly torn by the Ship, and I am bruised and beaten away—Sea, when you fling your Spray into my kingdom, I am not invaded.

(They understand obscurely that there was the Day when for the first time the Wind of God went rushing upon the Abyss, and the barren waters stirred, and *that* began which went beyond them, of which they could have no consciousness, and yet, it was seen that it was good. The Air, stooping upon the Sea, plunges strongly and gently into it, and a myriad tiny bubbles swirl intricately in all directions. The Sea, aspiring upwards, sends its uncountable drops, invisible from the outset, into the Air, and the Air absorbs them and sweetens itself and mends the tatters that the Ship has made and passes onwards in vast tides, though whence and whither you do not see.

Angels, understanding both the Sea and the Air in their unstirring thought, offer their Praise in voices indistinguishable from the Voice of Many Waters:

O Lord of every Sea,
To Thee the floods, to Thee
   The unthinking thunder of their voices raise :
What though the waves retract
Their showering cataract—
   Lord, was not all of this their due appointed
     Praise ?

Thou that dost guide the gale,
Nor shall Thy tempest fail
   All inarticulate to chant Thy Name.
The tattered, twisted Air
Itself exhales Thy Prayer—
   The sightless undulant Air reverting whence
     it came.

O Love, that hast no end—
O Dove divine, descend ;
   Turn into one great Font this barren Flood !
Thy gift of Life re-give ;
Let that which died, re-live ;
   Warm upon Nature's heart, O fostering Spirit,
     brood !

The interior of the Ship also is understood by the Angels. Our eyes would have seen many hundreds of men and women fast asleep; a few men moving to and fro with eyelids red from wakefulness and with tired lines round their lips; and the men working in the engine-room and the stoke-hole. All these are being understood by the Angels.

.   .   .   .   .

(The Stoke-Hole. You are standing at one end of a narrow passage about 7 ft. wide running right across the Ship. Down one side, the circular mouths of 10 furnaces. In the middle, the passage, about 18 ins. wide, through which you go to the perpendicular iron ladders reaching up towards the air. Opposite, another passage going into the other half of the Hole. A tangle of tubes, supports and machinery, all metal, is visible half-way up to the roof, but you can see no further because of the coal-dust suspended in the air. One or two dim electric lights: half the furnaces are shut; from the rest, which are open, a violent glare and roar proceeds, striking across the passage. At these, three men work incessantly. They are dressed in thin vests, wringing wet with sweat, which also streams in large drops down their faces and arms; they wear thick trousers and heavy boots. They have a rag of waste twisted round their middle. Some use caps with transparent green peaks, against the ferocious glare. They are not heavily muscular, but wiry; no spare flesh at all. Their faces scowl with concentration as they heave up the burning coal with long steel bars, or rake the fires so as to get rid of cinders. Instruments show upon dials the pressure of the steam. Another, a lad, 17 years old, incessantly wheels in barrow-loads of coal from a chamber, of which there are two, opening off the passage at either end; in these chambers you can be aware of the curving side of the ship on your left, and towering cliff-faces of coal in front and to your right. The wall, whether of steel or of coal, vanishes almost at once in the black powder that rises all the time: high up, a patch of luminous haze indicates that a lamp is burning there, but you only guess it. When the boy has brought his barrow in, he tilts the coal out, and smashes up the larger lumps with an enormous hammer. His features remain fixed in a positive grimace of concentration and with the effort needed to swing the hammer. The floor is heaped, at the moment, with piles of fresh coal, of scaldingly hot cinders, and black dust. You could not touch the iron floor with your feet bare. Torrents of air plunge down through ventilation-shafts, and seem icy by contrast: but you would say they crash down too violently, and spout back into the shafts or lose themselves in fierce eddies, lashing the dust into desperation, but leaving the Stoke-Hole in vertical layers of scorching heat and shivering cold. Two men are leaning back while their furnaces are shut; they have put the rags of waste round their necks and chew the ends of them, sweat-soddened and dust-caked as they are, for, you must chew something, else your mouth becomes too rigid with the coal-dust in it. Fortunately you can digest coal-dust. They also have fragments of cigarettes, soaked brown with sweat, which they light from burning cinders and puff at once or twice.)

JACK: You goin' ashore at Port Cheviot?

JIM: Cer'nly I'm going ashore. Ain't we layin' up for three days? Cer'nly I'm going.

JACK: Got a regular little home there?

JIM: Ah. Believe me. An' not a penny passed this side nor that.

JACK: Change from this dog's life.

JIM: Like hell it is! Dog's life? 'Tain't so human a life as a dog's.

JACK: Reckon it might be worse. I'd choose the Hole every time against the stewards.

JIM: Call us the dregs, they do. If we're dregs, they're the scum.

JACK: Ah. Crawling on their bellies for the tips. We don't get no tips.

JIM: See them two women what come down personally conducted, to see the 'orrid stokers? They didn't offer no tips. Not as I'd accept

79

it off of 'em. I ain't no exhibit. I'm a man, when all's said.

JACK: Huh ! course you'd accept of it. Reg'lar girl or not, you don't want to be takin' all the time and giving naught. That ain't no man's game, that.

JIM: Bin a machine down here so long I forgotten how to be a man.

(Jack shivers violently; in a moment his teeth chatter. He moves out of the current of air and goes close up against the furnace-door.)

JIM: Got a touch of malaria comin' on again ?

JACK: Something cruel.

JIM: Sit down 'ere. It's about time to do them fires. I'll do yourn.

JACK (*crouching down in the coal*): Well, I won't say no, Jim. You don't want me to thank you, Jim.

JIM: Better see the doc. to-morrow, mate.

JACK: I won't see no doc. Might make me go sick. I ain't going sick; nor I won't have no one working 6 hour watches instead of 4 on my account.

JIM: Ah ! They wouldn't mind.

JACK: I won't 'ave it. Bin too much o' that already. Cruel on the 'ands. Look at young Joe what had festering hands last week and had to lay up—four days, weren't it ? And us havin' to work a 6 hour lay. We'd be doin' it still, if

80

it weren't for him workin' again already with them gloves on.

JIM: Cer'nly he has pluck. But he didn't ought to wear no gloves. 'E can't sweat proper; least-ways the sweat don't work out proper through them gloves. Start festering again, he will. Ah—look over there. . . .

(A blazing piece of coal has flown out and set fire to the trousers of a man working at the far end. He does not notice it at first because the thick cloth, overlapping the boot, just smoulders. Then the flame shoots up and licks his leg. Jim runs over and crushes it out in his hands. He returns.

JIM: Pity it wasn't his arms. Then 'e'd take no harm. Sweat the burn out. But workin' with a burn beneath them breeches. . . . Can you wonder ? *Can* you wonder ?

JACK: Can I wonder what ?

JIM: Why, when we gets ashore ! Anything to forget. You see. Young Perce'll be on the game, this time, same as us. Get drunk, too, most like; miss his ship and be sacked the Company.

JACK: I'll keep him along with me. I ain't got nothing reg'lar.

JIM: Ah ! don't you sacrifice yerself. Got to learn, ain't he ? Same as the rest of us.

JACK: I caught him yesterday, the tears trickling down his face.

81

JIM: That weren't no tears. Sweat, most like. Take him, and you learn him to be a man.

JACK: He'd be sorry after.

JIM: Gar ! there ain't no room for being sorry in this life.

(A shovel is rattled violently on the iron of a furnace. JACK and JIM go to see to their own fires. After a while, JACK lies down on the hot floor. The two unoccupied men take him under the armpits and hoist him up the ladder.)

THE MEN: Best get him up quick.—Chuck hisself overboard, if 'e ain't careful, like pore old Sammy last trip.—Ah, the sharks got *him* all right, long before we'd put about even. Curse this 'ere Red Sea. We'd all be overboard if it wasn't for the rum.

(In the further coal-chamber, two figures of men can dimly be descried; one kneeling, the other sitting on the coal.)

THE KNEELING MAN: It's s'long ago I don't rightly know how to begin. . . . No; not since I left school. . . . Couldn't you ask me the questions and me answer ? . . . I forget the I confess: could you say it in my name, like ? . . .

THE PRAYER OF EARTH: Misereatur tui Omnipotens Deus . . . Dominus Noster Iesus Christus te absolvat . . . deinde ego te absolvo . . . Passio Domini nostri . . .

merita Beatae Mariae . . . quidquid boni
feceris et mali sustinueris . . .

THE HEART OF HEAVEN: Again, again, my soul
doth magnify the Lord, and my spirit rejoices.
I, ever Thy handmaiden; he, once more Thy
servant. Once more he, in his generation,
will name me Blessed. . . . My new-born son
—to me you have " offered yourself without
any reserve," and have consecrated to me this
night your eyes, your ears, your mouth, your
heart and your whole person. Since you
belong to me, my dear, dear son, I will treat
you indeed as my own and my possession.

(Her voice turns Godwards, praying during that
" now " which shall last for him until the hour
of his death.)

Who is like to God ? Satan, you who said
you would not serve, go back from this man,
God's servant, for in the day of tremendous
Judgment I will defend him.

(And he, too, turns to God.)

Behold again the Death of the eternal Lamb
of God, having conquered death in the endur-
ing duel. O Thou that art the soul's one
Bridegroom, I, Thy friend, am standing at
Thy side to share in this night's joy !

With my eternal Keys, I have this night shut
hell and opened heaven. Ah, to whom else
should he have gone, Thou whom I love,

save Thee ? Thou hast the words of ever-
lasting life, and this night hast spoken them.
My son ! My joy, my crown ! What to pray,
or how, you had forgotten; but all the while
the Spirit, given to you in baptism, was joining
hands with the weakness of your soul, and
praying in you with prayers that were beyond
all words: and He, who scrutinized the innermost of your heart, understood what was
the meaning of His Spirit. . . . Now to the
Father of Our Lord, Jesus Christ, be gratitude;
and, for His servants, grace, and peace in
the most Holy Ghost.

(In heaven, the coal-hole is seen to be radiant
with the Light that had appeared too inaccessible.
The Ship proceeds on its way, glowing with gentle
glory. The Waves reflect it; and the Winds are
in tune with it.)

Ah, for a space, your hymn
    Hush, and withhold the triumph-song of heaven!
Angels, Archangels, Thrones, and Seraphim,
    Adore in secret, silently adore—
To this one human heart such grace was given
    That hardly earth needs heaven any more
To amplify its hymn!

Suffer our souls to kneel
    Deep lost within their ecstasy and dark;
Un-needing now to speak or think or feel,
    Un-noticing if even your voices cease:

The Dove returns, returns into its Ark—
    A man by God is gathered into peace—
Ah, heaven! I pray you, kneel.

THE KNEELING MAN (*standing up*): Gee, I feel better now! Gee, I am that happy. I'd thought, never again. I'd never manage it no more! (*He brushes the back of his hand across his eyes.*) This ain't sweat! No, and if anyone had told me I'd have tears of joy in my eyes to-night, I'd have mocked him. But gee! Anyways it can't make me look more of a zebbera than what I did. Well, I've said me Our Father and 'Ail Mary right here agin the bunker; an' now I've got to pray for me mates, 'ave I? What price them laughing if they knew?

(He returns to his fire; and as his rake or his slice swing rhythmically in and out, the names " Jack," " Jim," " Joe," " Sammy," " Perce," rise like globes of quiet fire through the cloudy splendour amid which the transfigured ship proceeds.

At 4 o'clock, the men go up and cross the well-deck to their peak forrard. Twelve of them sleep there, bunks one above the other. Nothing is at right angles, owing to the slope of the ship's side inwards, and its curve towards the bows; when the sea is high, it spouts through the portholes and soaks their bedding. There is room, therefore, for bunks arranged in about a third of a circle; a plank runs lengthways, on which they eat and beneath which they stow their boxes; and a narrow gangway goes behind two more bunks. The supports of the roof are hung with birdcages. Most of the 12—4 watch comes into this particular room; a couple of men have left their bunks to go down to the 4—8 watch; Jack is lying under a heap of sacks, clothes and anything his companions could put hands on. The men who have been down the hole at once drink mugs of tea that had been left there in a kettle. Then they strip for washing, wrap a towel round them, and prepare to go to the bath-house. They notice that JOCK, MICK and TEDDIE have drunk no tea.)

JIM: What's come to you three?

   (They look at one another and say nothing.)

JIM: What's come to you? Ain't you drinking no tea?

JOCK: Say, Jim, could you see that the pails are kept on the far side of the bath-house so's the water'll run straight out without floodin' the whole place?

JIM: Say, Jock, what 'n hell are you talking of? What's this about them pails?

JOCK: Me and some of me mates is Roman Catholic and we're holdin' Mass in the wash-house when we've done cleaning, and we want to keep the near side dry for to have it on.

JIM: Gawd ! Religion in the wash-house ? You preaching the sermon, Jock ? Come 'ere, Jock. What you talkin' about ? You ain't never going to hold a service in the middle o' the night in the wash-house ?

JOCK: Ye—eh. And we ain't having no argument about it, but we ask civil if you'd keep the near side dry. (*He goes out.*)

JIM (to BERT): What's come to 'im ? Who did ever hear the like. No one ain't said nothing to *me* about them going to hold no service.

BERT: Well, you'd hardly expect of 'em to make a song about it right here in the peak. Then the Catholics is secret men. But we all seen the priest comin' down and talkin' civil to the lot of us, and I reckon he's give 'em the order.

JIM: I don't hold with no such thing. If religion ain't free on this blooming ship, what is ? Stopping us poor devils having their tea and getting 'em out for to say psalms when due for their sleep.

(Bert shrugs his shoulders and gets on to his bunk.)

BERT: Well, nobody's stopped you having *your* tea, s'far's I can see; and no one ain't stopping me having me own sleep. (*He rolls over. Jim sits staring.*)

(After a while, the men return from the bathroom, quite clean save for the black rims round

87

their eyelids which take days to remove. They dress hastily and return to the bath-house.

The ship has a slight list, and all the water has run away leaving the bath-house dry. An altar has been put up against the wall at the extreme end of the ship. The electric light is dim; but men huddle beneath it to read from their Seamen's Prayer Books. It is August 6th; and the priest says the Mass of the Transfiguration by the light of his two candles.)

Introibo ad Altare Dei . . .

THE AIR: Thy radiant Light, O Lord, has shone to the end of the earth. . . .

THE SEA: The solid earth has stirred—the earth is trembling. . . .

THE THOUGHTS IN THE HEARTS OF THE MEN: How dear is Thy dwelling, O Lord, Lord of my strength. . . . My heart was sick for this. . . . My soul, without knowing it, was fainting for this Thy royal room. . . .

THE ACKNOWLEDGEMENT FROM HEAVEN, THAT CONTINUES VOICELESSLY THROUGHOUT THE MASS: O My Son, these, too, are My beloved sons, with whom I am well-pleased.

THE SOULS IN PURGATORY, FLOCKING INVISIBLY ROUND THE SIDES OF THE SHIP: Lift up your gates for us, too, O you princes! Open to us, too, the immortal doors, that with the King of Glory we may enter as His retinue. Pray for us, you favoured among His people, that we may be made worthy of the promises of Christ.

(At the Offertory, the iron floor of the bath-house becomes golden, and is the Paten upon which the Grains are placed that are about to be kneaded into one Bread of God. The sloping walls curve up into the Chalice, within which will be made the Wine that gladdens the lips of God.)

.   .   .   .   .

O God, who hast set the work of these Thy servants amid the fires of this Ship, grant that their souls may never be scorched by the fires of sin or hell.

God, who by the wood of Thy Son's Cross and its iron nails and the Red Sea of His Passion, dost save Thy children from their enemies, carry these men safely to the harbour of their desire.

O Lord, who camest walking over the waters amid the storm, so that they took Thee for a phantom, come in the manifold Reality of Thy Presence into this place, into these hearts, taking away fear, granting peace, establishing them in hope!

.   .   .   .   .

The Sanctus Bell rings. The SHIP, as though aware of its majestic destiny now imminent, goes forward evenly into the night, and upon it Heaven concentrates its watch. The Universe holds its breath when the Warning Bell is rung; there is a globe of silence within the creaking bulkheads and the frothing of the water against the walls; and the men are within the silence. The Consecration. Hereupon the whole Ship is an Altar, with its two candles illuminating the Sea beyond any imaginable horizon, and shining till they mingle with the stars, those Stars, I mean, whose light shall have no setting. Instead of the little Crucifix, Christ stands at the head of the Ship that is now at the world's head. The Sea, the Winds, the Ship and its Engines, the Men, the Mass, proceed magnificently towards God, to whom at that moment there is being given, through Christ, along with Christ, in Christ, all Honour and Glory.

The Glory, that had gone widening out from the Ship, a streaming Glory embracing the whole world and eternally spreading forth through Heaven, has now altered its current and is setting back towards man. *Domine, non sum dignus*. The men get up from their huddle under the lamp, kneel once more in a row, and receive Holy Communion. *O res mirabilis—manducat Dominum—pauper, servus, et humilis*. Very soon after that they return silently to their peak. For a while, the Sea itself is hushed, and accepts from heaven upon its heart the brooding of God's Dove.

.   .   .   .   .

Now quenched the Candles. Now the Cloud that shone
   Into its own Heart re-absorbs its splendour.
Now fold I, Lord, Thy linen; and upon
   Thy Mount is silence. I to Thee surrender
These hearts that seemed, just then, my very own—
Take them, O Thou remaining here alone.

Now human sleep descends on human thought.
   Serene above your heads resumes his station
Each Guardian Angel. You, to whom Christ has brought
   In one brief hour all life's transfiguration—
I kiss your feet; upon my eyes I place
Your hands that He anointed with such grace.

XXVII

ELEVATION[1]

I LIFT this Bread,
And lift therewith myself, the world, and Thee.
    Hast Thou not said:
" I, lifted up, will draw the universe to Me " ?

        O heavenward Cup !
The drops that redden in Thy tiny bowl
        Could swallow up
The oceans undulant from pole to utmost pole.

        Then no demur,
Weak fingers, to exalt the enormous load!
        Thou Christopher—
All heaven and earth sustain thee that dost carry
    God.

[1] This has been set to music by Fr. L. Rowlands, O.S.F.C.

XXVIII

GUM TREES

WHEN I wake up at the flick of the breeze,
What are you whispering, great Gum Trees?
Why are you making that curious noise?
What are you saying to little Bush-Boys?
  " Stick to it, sonny! you stick to it, stick to it!
  What if the wind has a bit of a flick to it?
  Up with you! tackle the work of the day!
  Tackle it, stick to it—come what may."

What must I stick to, you big Gum Trees?
Yellow tree, white tree, and red as you please?
Pale—tall—trunks, like ghosts in the dark.
You can't even stick tight to your bark!
  " Stick to it, kiddie; go down on your knees;
  Whether it scorches or whether it freeze!
  Stick to your prayers when the morning is gold;
  Stick to them tight when the night turns cold."

How shall I stick to it, all of the day?
Mummy is busy and Daddy's away.
What shall I do, when there's nothing to do?
What's the advice I am getting from you?
  " Stick to your lessons, when lessons are right.
  Stick to your duty when Dad's out of sight.
  Couldn't you learn a bit? help a bit? work a bit?
  Lads like you wouldn't fancy to shirk a bit!"

How shall I stick to it once I'm a man?
" Sonny, dear sonny—we all of us *can*.
Harder the task when you're aiming more high:
Manhood is kind to the boy that'll try."

(*The music sinks half a tone or so.*)

What shall I do when it's time to grow old?
What shall I do when the world turns cold?
What shall I do, when the mist's in my eye?
What shall I feel, when the call is to die?
" Dear, dear son—don't *you* be afraid of it!
Life'll be worth what you and Christ made of it.
Can't you guess how Christ'll stick fast to you?
How Christ holds to the last of the last of you? "

(*It rises again.*)

Big big Gums, I'll stick to it, stick to it!
Work? I promise you—I shall go slick to it.
Long limp leaves, I hear what you sing to me;
Dear dim trees, I take what you bring to me.
Stick to it, stick to it, stick to it, stick to it!
If there's a building, let *me* add a brick to it!
Thanks be to God for the voice of the Gum;
Let me be faithful whatever may come.

XXIX

THE ENGLISH BABY ASKS . . .[1]

"OUT in Australia, oh *what* did you see?
    Little bears climbing around on a tree?
Kangaroos coming for afternoon tea?
Did you see babies exactly like me?"

Out in Australia, my darling, it's true—
There are dozens of babies exactly like you:
All of them eating the very same food;
All, I am certain, exactly as good!

"But didn't you meet with such different things—
Birds that could laugh at you—fishes with wings!
If you've got nothing surprising to say,
What is the good of your going away?"

Well, there were children I never did see
(Which was a great disappointment to me);
Little Bush Babies so sturdy and brown—
Babes in the Bush that have never seen town!

"But why—oh but why—do they live in a bush?
What if an elephant gave them a push?

[1] One of Australia's most difficult problems is the education of children whose homes are far out in the Bush and separated by great distances. Of course, for the Catholic the problem becomes a hundred times more anxious. The Rev. Dr. J. McMahon, of Perth, inaugurated the system of teaching by correspondence, with its many ramifications.

Who is it puts them to sleep in their nest?
What do they talk like? and how are they
   dressed?"

Ah, but Bush Babies aren't just what they sound!
Nor are there elephants roaming around.
Still, there are lizards as big as your arm;
Yes, and a snake can do plenty of harm.

Some little girls wear a calico smock;
Some of them manage a regular frock:
And if it's a boy, well, he frequently wears
His father's big breeches braced up to his ears!

Still, they are often less lucky than you;
Their fathers and mothers have so much to do!
And who is it helps little babies like them?
Who but the Reverend Doctor Mac *M.?*

He and the little black nuns and the brown
Bring the Bush Babies right up to the town;
Give them a dip in the surf and the sea;
Find them some lollies for afternoon tea.

Teach them their lessons out under the sun;
Play with them after the lessons are done:
Play with them, pray with them, sing them to
   sleep—
Wrap them up safe for Our Lady to keep.

" Wouldn't I like to go back there with you!
Surely there's something I'd manage to do!
I'm sure that Australians have never *seen* tea!
Couldn't I bring some, from you and from me ? "

Well—*tea* the Australians possibly know—
But most of the babies have never seen snow!
And to-day is so hot—will you trust what I say ?—
That I hardly can write; yet it's Christmas Day.

So, if you will ask Him, the Baby Divine
Will bring to Bush Babies your presents and mine;
And Mary, the Bush-Mothers' Mother, and His,
Will lift to their babies *her* Baby to kiss.

POPLAR LEAVES AND SEAWEED